MISS LIBERTY

MISS LIBERTY
First Lady of the World

By June Behrens

ℂℙ CHILDRENS PRESS ®

CHICAGO

ABOUT THE AUTHOR

JUNE BEHRENS has a rich background of experience from which to draw in meeting the reading needs of children. For many years a reading specialist in one of California's largest public school systems, she has also done extensive graduate work. A native Californian, Mrs. Behrens was graduated from the University of California at Santa Barbara and obtained her Master's degree from the University of Southern California. She also holds a Credential in Early Childhood Education. She is the author of many books for young children, ranging in subject matter from Colonial history to contemporary biography. She lives with her husband in Rancho Palos Verde near Los Angeles.

Picture Acknowledgements:

Roloc Color Slides—Cover, 10, 13 (right), 17 (top right), 19 (top right), 21, 23 (2 photos), 24 (right), 28 (top left), 30

Nawrocki Stock Photo:
© Ulrike Welsch—1, 11 (bottom), 17
© William S. Nawrock—9 (top right), 13 (left)
© Robert Amft—28

Hillstrom Stock Photo:
©Tom McCarthy—2
© Karen Kent—9, 12

Historical Pictures Service—3, 8, 12 (bottom right), 16, 19 (top left, bottom left, bottom right), 20, 22, 24 (left)

Photri—5, 11 (top), 15 (3 photos), 26, 32

Cameramann International, Ltd.—6-7

United Press International—27

Ellis Island Foundation—25

Design by Karen A. Yops

Library of Congress Cataloging-in-Publication Data

Behrens, June.
  Miss Liberty: First Lady of the world.
  Summary: Describes the conception, construction in France, erection in New York Harbor, and recent renovation of the tallest statue of modern times.
    1. Statue of Liberty (New York, N.Y.)—Juvenile literature. [1. Statue of Liberty (New York, N.Y.) 2. National monuments. 3. Statues] I. Title.
  F128.64.L6B44 1986   730' .92'4   86-2320
  ISBN 0-516-03295-X

When the head of the Statue of Liberty was completed
in 1878, Frederic Bartholdi's dream of uniting the
French and Americans in friendship began to come true.

The most beautiful lady in
America is one hundred years old.
Americans celebrate with parades,
street festivals, and special events.

Ships salute Miss Liberty. A postage stamp (top right) honors the statue's designer.

People from far away countries come to the birthday party. Millions watch the fireworks over New York harbor. Tall sailing ships from around the world pass to salute her.

What a birthday party for Miss Liberty!

For almost one hundred years Miss Liberty held her torch high. But her framework had weakened. Her copper skin was corroded. She had loose and missing parts. The years had taken their toll. Miss Liberty was in danger.

Americans built the granite pedestal for Miss Liberty at a cost of $250,000. Spaces were left over the entrance to display shields of the United States and France.

A call went out to help Miss Liberty. The people of America heard that call. Money poured in from every state. People from other parts of the world helped to repair and restore the great lady.

Her skin was cleaned. She was given a new torch. Loose and missing bolts were replaced. Repairs were made inside, outside, and on the base of Miss Liberty. She was made new and strong again for her hundredth birthday party.

The rare 1880 photo (above) shows workmen at the Paris plant shaping copper sheets to place over wood impressions that were taken from the large plaster model standing behind them. Repairs on the statue (right) were begun in 1984.

By 1918 magazines such as the *Literary Digest* (left)
were appealing to the immigrants' experience of freedom.

Miss Liberty could be called the
First Lady of the World. She is,
perhaps, the most famous statue
known. The great lady has welcomed
millions of people from around the
world.

Opposite: Miss Liberty was designed as a lighthouse to guide
ships into the harbor and light the way to a land of opportunity.

Miss Liberty is the tallest statue of modern times. The colossal lady and her pedestal are 305 feet high. She weighs 225 tons.

In the pedestal of Miss Liberty is the American Museum of Immigration. It was opened in 1972. The museum tells the story of the millions of people who came from other lands to live in America. Many say these people, called immigrants, made America what it is.

The Statue of Liberty holds the torch of freedom. The tablet in her left hand is dated July 4, 1776, the date of the Declaration of Independence. At her feet are broken chains, the promise of liberty. In her crown are seven rays, or spikes. They stand for the seven continents and the seven seas.

About 22 million immigrants came into the United States between 1890 and 1900. Most people came from Poland, Russia, Italy, Spain, and Greece. Before leaving for their new homes, people were checked for disease. Although most immigrants could not read or write English, religious groups often gave them bibles.

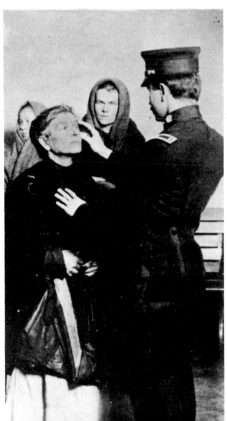

Frederic Bartholdi began work on Liberty at the age of 37. By the time the statue was dedicated in 1886, Bartholdi had devoted nearly 20 years of his life to its construction.

Miss Liberty came to America from France. Frenchman Edward de Laboulaye has been called her "father." One night at a dinner, he and friends talked about a gift to the United States. It would be from the people of France to celebrate their great friendship with the people of America. It should be given in 1876, when the United States celebrated one hundred years of independence.

French sculptor Frederic Auguste Bartholdi had an idea. The gift would be a statue of a gigantic Greek goddess holding a torch. He would call his statue *Liberty Enlightening the World*. It should be placed in New York harbor.

Opposite: The head of Miss Liberty was built to hold 40 visitors. It can be reached by climbing a spiral staircase from the pedestal.

Edward de Laboulaye called on the people of France to pay for this gift. Cities and villages, adults and children gave money. In the United States, money was collected to build the base or pedestal for the statue.

With the needed money, Bartholdi started his work. First, he built models. Then he enlarged his models. Alexandre Eiffel helped with the strong iron supports for the statue.

Bartholdi and his men worked for years. Copper sheets were pressed into wooden patterns and hammered into shape by the workmen. The head of the statue was finished in 1878. People at the World's Fair in Paris marveled at its size.

Opposite: After its completion, the statue was assembled in Paris to make sure all the pieces fit before shipping them to the United States; Miss Liberty (top right) being carefully reassembled in America; Framework for the hand of Liberty (bottom right)

FOOT AND PART OF TORCH

THE FACE

THE FLAME

19

Miss Liberty arrived aboard the French transport boat, the Isère, escorted by the finest naval procession New Yorkers had ever seen.

In Paris, on July 4, 1884, the finished statue was given to the people of the United States. Then it was taken apart and packed for shipping. A train of seventy cars carried it to a ship for the trip to America.

The Statue of Liberty arrived in New York harbor in June, 1885. People watched as the statue was put together again. Miss Liberty on her pedestal became one of the largest sculptures in the history of the world. Her home was on Bedloe's Island, inside the star-shaped walls of old Fort Wood.

Newspapers in 1885 claimed that it would take four weeks to unload all the pieces of the statue carefully packed in 85 crates in the hull of the Isère (opposite).

A public holiday was declared in honor of the formal installation of the statue. Crowds waving American and French flags packed into Madison Square for a big parade.

On October 28, 1886, President Grover Cleveland and French leaders met. They sealed their ties of friendship with the dedication of *Liberty Enlightening the World.* Ships crowded New York harbor. People came from everywhere to see this grand statue. At sunset the torch burned for all to see. No one cared that the gift was ten years late!

Ellis Island, named after Samuel Ellis, the original owner, is about one mile southwest of the city of Manhattan. Right: The medical examining room at Ellis Island

In 1924 Miss Liberty was made a national monument. Bedloe's Island was renamed Liberty Island in 1956. Now the National Park Service takes care of her. Liberty is one part of the Statue of Liberty National Monument. Ellis Island is the other.

Ellis Island was opened as an immigration station in 1892. More than 12 million immigrants came to live in America between 1892 and 1954. Shiploads passed Miss Liberty on their way to Ellis Island. Ellis

Immigrants (left) waiting to be accepted into America. Right: The kitchen at Ellis Island

Island was their first stop in the United States. It was there they learned whether they could stay in this new land.

Miss Liberty became a beacon of friendship. She was there to welcome them. She stirred their hearts. She inspired them with new hopes and dreams.

If Miss Liberty could talk, what stories she would tell! She has ushered in a century of technology.

Miss Liberty's new torch was built, as was the original, by a French Company. Using the corroded torch as a model, artisians shaped its exterior surface by hammering the metal's undersurface. This embossing technique, known as repoussé forming, was used to build the original statue.

Technology is the science of the practical or industrial arts. When Miss Liberty came to America in 1885, people did not know much about technology.

In her time men have walked on the moon. People can move from one part of the earth to another in hours. They know at once what is happening anywhere in the world. They know the secrets of the atom.

Immigrants waiting to be transferred from Ellis Island to Manhattan around 1890

Miss Liberty might tell about the many changes during her time span. There were changes in people, who moved from farms to cities. They found new ways of growing food and producing goods in great numbers. People now live longer, thanks to the science of medicine.

Her stories would be about growth and progress. They would be about great events and the joys of new discoveries.

Not only immigrants seek refuge in the light of Lady Liberty. In 1978 Native Americans, supported by Muhammad Ali (center), protested the taking of their land through United States treaties.

Miss Liberty is more than a statue of iron and copper. She stands for "Liberty Enlightening the World" with her torch of freedom. She is the symbol of our country's greatness. Miss Liberty is First Lady of the World.

STATUE OF LIBERTY

1865	Edward de Laboulaye proposes a monument to French and American friendship
1871	Sculptor Frederic Auguste Bartholdi has an idea for a statue, *Liberty Enlightening the World*
1875	Bartholdi completes first plaster model of statue
1877	Bedloe's Island chosen as the site for the statue
1878	At Paris World's Fair, the head of Miss Liberty is exhibited
1883	Poet Emma Lazarus writes THE NEW COLOSSUS
1884	Bartholdi completes statue
1885	Statue arrives in New York harbor aboard ship *Isère*
1886	October 28, President Grover Cleveland dedicates *Liberty Enlightening the World*
1924	Statue of Liberty declared a National Monument by President Calvin Coolidge
1933	Liberty becomes part of U.S. Department of the Interior, administered by National Park Service
1936	President Franklin Roosevelt presides over celebration of Miss Liberty's fiftieth birthday
1942-45	Miss Liberty's torch is blacked out during World War II
1956	Bedloe's Island is renamed Liberty Island by approval of Congress and President Dwight D. Eisenhower
1965	Ellis Island becomes part of Statue of Liberty National Monument
1972	Dedication of American Museum of Immigration
1982	Centennial Commission appointed by President Ronald Reagan to restore the Statue of Liberty
1986	Statue of Liberty centennial

Opposite: Frederic Bartholdi fell in love with and married Miss Jeanne Emilie Baheux, his model for the Statue of Liberty.

VITAL STATISTICS OF
THE STATUE OF LIBERTY

Height from base to torch	151 ft. 1 in.
Steps in statue from base to torch	171 steps
Height from base of foundation to torch	305 ft. 1 in.
Heel to head	111 ft. 1 in.
Height of torch	21 ft.
Length of hand	16 ft. 5 in.
Index finger	8 ft.
Circumference of finger at 2nd joint	3 ft. 6 in.
Size of fingernail	13 × 10 in.
Chin to cranium	17 ft. 3 in.
Head thickness from ear to ear	10 ft.
Distance across eye	2 ft. 6 in.
Length of nose	4 ft. 6 in.
Length of right arm	42 ft.
Greatest thickness of right arm	12 ft.
Greatest thickness of waist	35 ft.
Width of mouth	3 ft.
Length of tablet	23 ft. 7 in.
Width of tablet	13 ft. 7 in.
Thickness of tablet	2 ft.
Height of granite pedestal	89 ft.
Height of foundation	65 ft.
Steps in pedestal	167 steps
Windows in crown	25 windows
Rays of diadem (representing the seven seas and seven continents)	7
Inscription on tablet in left hand commemorating Declaration of Independence	July 4, 1776 in Roman numerals
Weight of copper used in statue	100 tons
Weight of iron used in statue	125 tons
Total weight of statue	225 tons
Copper sheeting covering statue (thickness varies because of hammer forming)	⅛ to 3/32 in. thick

THE NEW COLOSSUS

Emma Lazarus

Not like the brazen giant of Greek fame,
With conquering limbs astride from land to land;
Here at our sea-washed, sunset gates shall stand
A mighty woman with a torch, whose flame
Is the imprisoned lightning, and her name
Mother of Exiles. From her beacon-hand
Glows world-wide welcome; her mild eyes command
The air-bridged harbor that twin cities frame.
"Keep ancient lands, your storied pomp!" cries she
With silent lips. "Give me your tired, your poor,
Your huddled masses yearning to breathe free,
The wretched refuse of your teeming shore.
Send these, the homeless, tempest-tost to me,
I lift my lamp beside the golden door!"